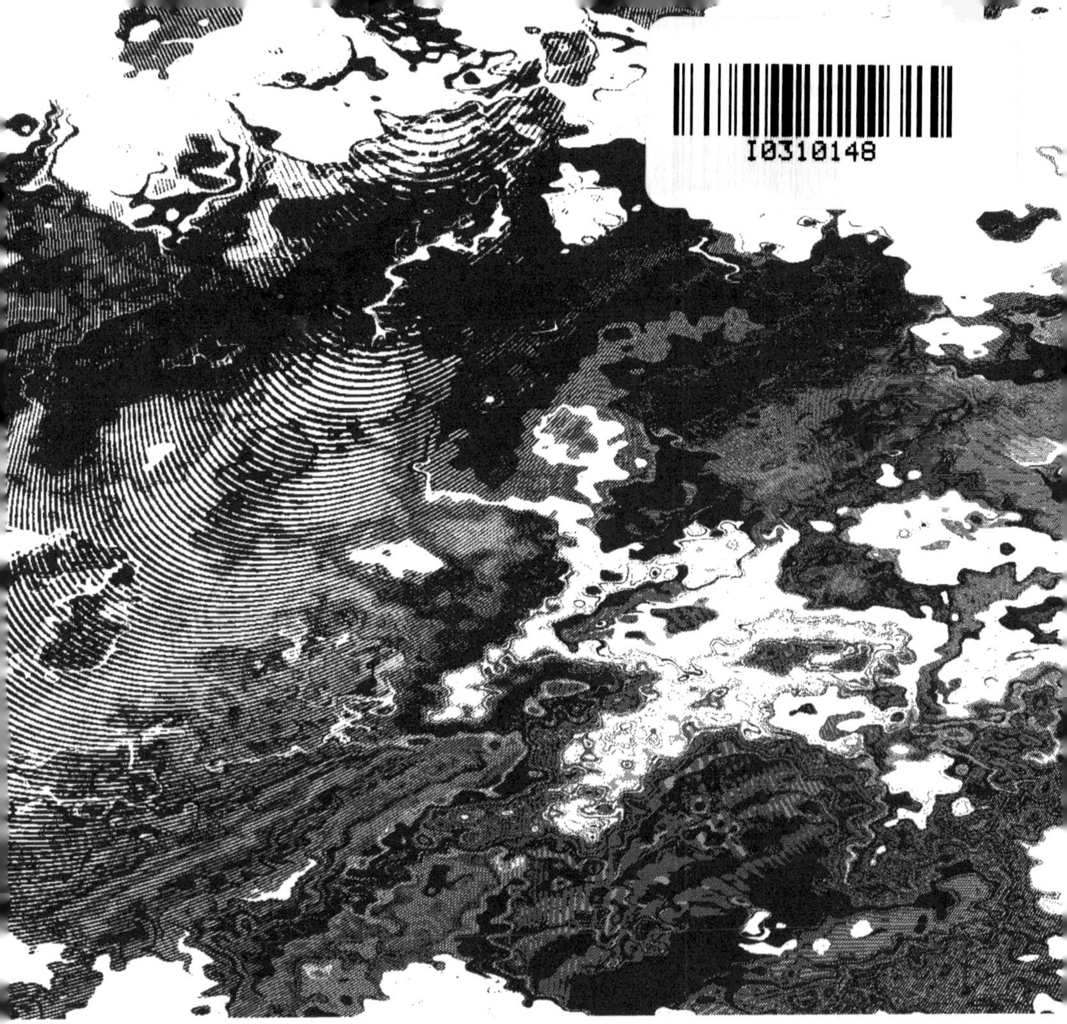

AN EXCHANGE IN DEMONOLOGY   ;
IMPROVEMENT OF   THE SELF    AND OTHERS

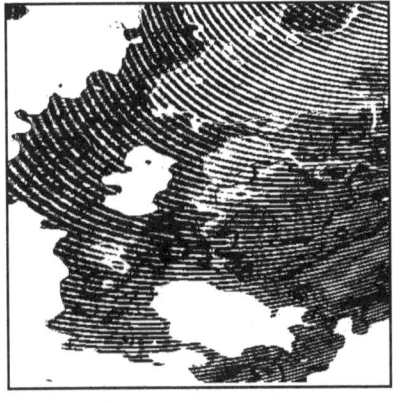 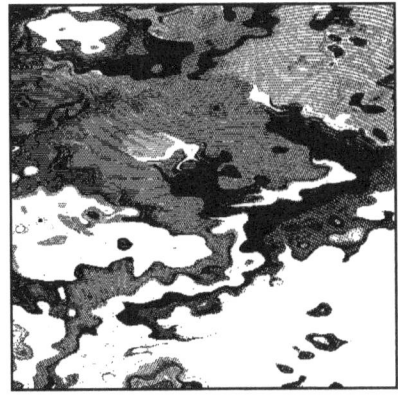

BY   SENIA HARDWICK

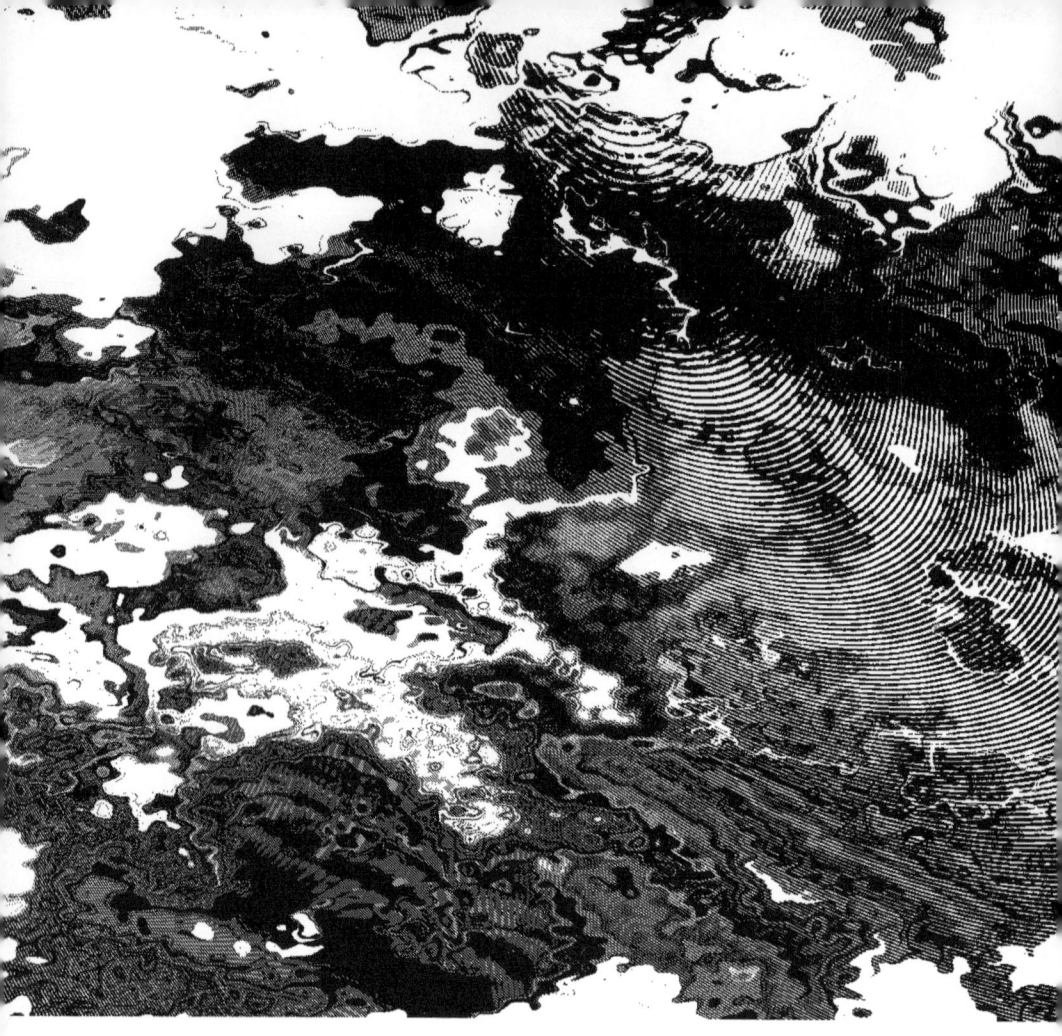

AN EXCHANGE IN DEMONOLOGY: THREE ZINES
CREATIVE COMMONS
SENIA HARDWICK 2022
IN COLLABORATION WITH CLOAK.WTF
ISBN: 978-0-578-28555-9

Introduction to Erotic Demonology and the Ars Goetia

Or, When Hating Your Hobbies So Hard You Contact the Astral Plane

Brought to you by Pyxis the Navigator

Introduction to Erotic Demonology and the Ars Goetia

THIS TEXT IS CREATIVE COMMONS // GIVE THIS TO EVERYONE

🛈 These instructions will provide a brief overview to the philosophical principles of what you are doing and what sort of invocations and history you need to be aware of. The rituals included are designed for President level demons in the Ars Goetia/Lesser Key of Solomon and are largely informed by a mixture of Crowley, neopaganism, and medieval practices.

Whether or not said demons are truly real in the literal sense of a metaphorical or psychedelic experience, please exercise safety with regards to the legality of any practices in your place or residence. Take the psychological and spiritual depths of your travel and experiences seriously. The author is not responsible for any harm suffered from a lack of preparation or ignoring instructions provided.

Inviting any entity into one's space (or any experience one perceives as such) is a significant task. These instructions are tailored to the psychology and personal metaphors of a specific recipient and so are constructed for maximum effectiveness for said individual. With some research, one can modify these constructions to better reflect one's own profile.

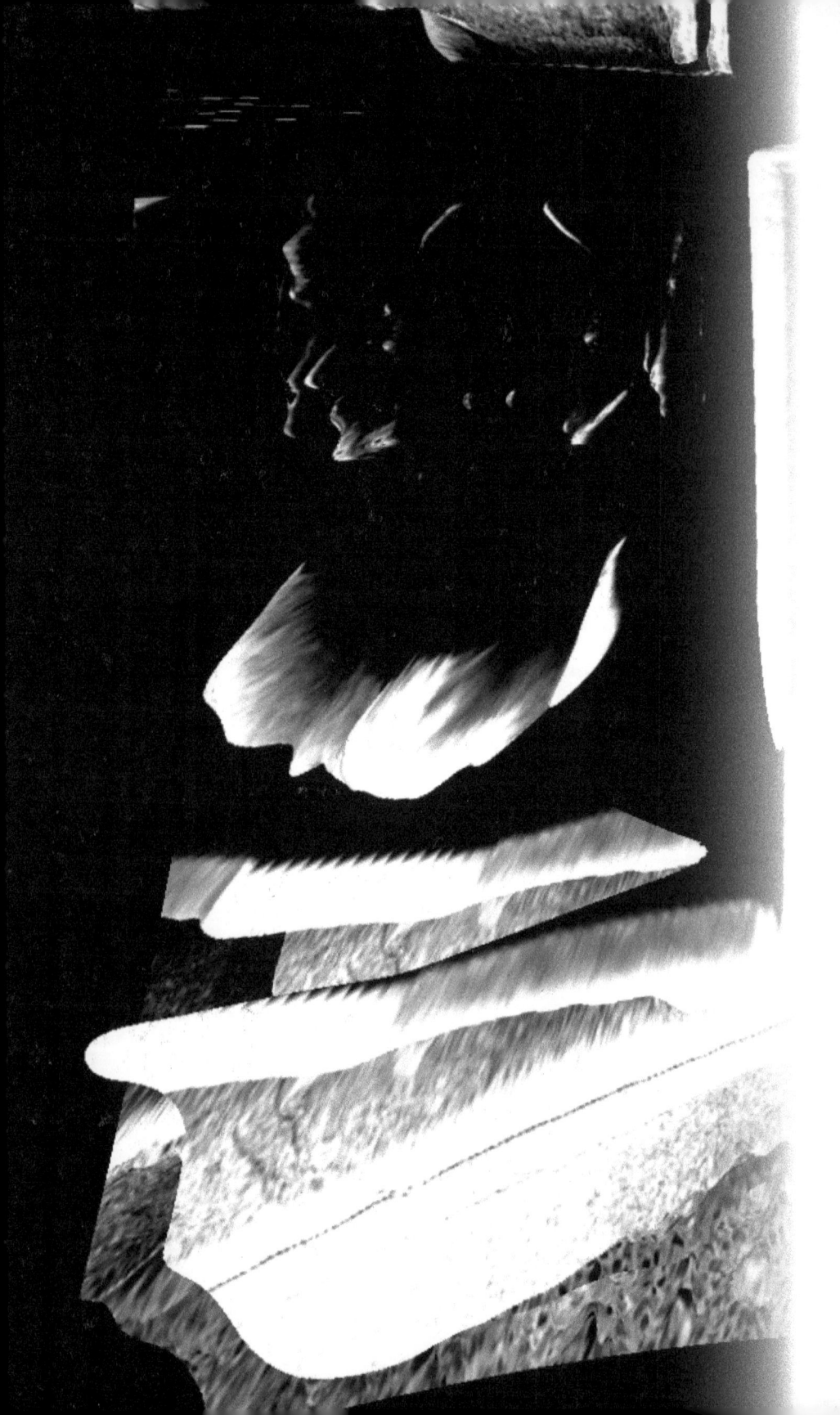

The Lesser Key of Solomon, also known as *Lemegeton Clavicula Salomonis* or simply *Lemegeton*, is an anonymous grimoire on demonology. It was compiled in the mid-17th century, mostly from materials a couple of centuries older. It is divided into five books—the Ars Goetia, Ars Theurgia-Goetia, Ars Paulina, Ars Almadel, and Ars Notoria.

- Wikipedia

Some cool historical notes are that this is from a period of time where acceptable and unacceptable forms of magic were considered a real and studied practice. Goetia, or the summoning of demons and spirits, was generally considered a negative practice as opposed to alchemy or other more benevolent forms.

Crowley's version of the text can be found for free online *here*.

Here's some miscellaneous thoughts I have on the matter of magic and ritual and what we are actually doing when preforming these rites:

- Whether or not demons exist is irrelevant. This is about manipulating your relationship with and experience of reality.

- Reclaiming demon worship from Christian-informed practices is politically radical because of the way the tradition appropriates various non-Christian theology and distorts it. For people outside Christianity to instead claim these traditions as our own and choose to ignore whether Christ or god have any relationship to these entities at all and not even assigning Christianity the role of something to be refused devalues it as an ideological system.

- Ritual practice and the senses are the prime ways to tap into one's spiritual being.

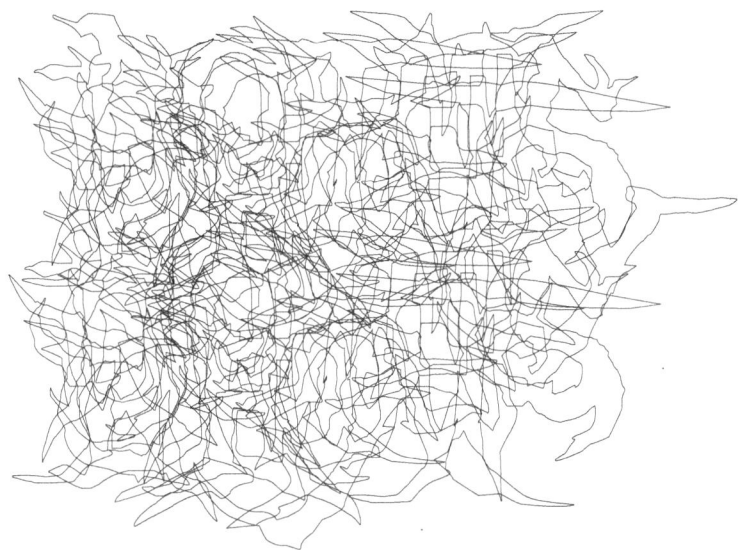

Some notes on what Crowley emphasizes in building a ritual space that I actually think are useful and which I have combined with my own study of a variety of fields:

- Ritual should include all of the following senses: sight, sound, smell, taste, touch, mind.

- Refusal or expansion of the ego or boundaries of the self is a source of power.

- Eroticism and the presence in one's sensation and feeling is a source of power. I have thoughts on how my stances compare and differ from the following essay by Audre Lorde, but she and Gloria Anzaldúa both deserve credit as writers who have pushed me in this direction:

    1. *The Uses of the Erotic by Lorde*

    2. *Borderlands/La Frontera*

- I don't think god's name or invoking it is particularly important and so I will not include it as such. If you want to say a prayer to an entity that matters to you go nuts, but there is frankly no need.

PERFORMING

What You'll Need:

- [ ] a small pot of tea and a small vessel to drink from
- [ ] floor space
- [ ] time undisturbed
- [ ] salt

Additionally recommended items:

- [ ] a personally scaled micro dose of a preferred psychedelic. I do not feel comfortable recommending dosages as this is incredibly personal. I do strongly recommend consulting *Erowid* for information regarding safety, complications, dosing, and experiences.

- [ ] A candle or other item of personal value to be used and given. For the sake of this personalized ritual, the caster is lighting and using a candle which holds significance to them. The gift of one's physical submission to the summoned force is actual for the gratification of the caster, and thus does not count as a true offering. Burned herbs, a small token, etc. are also acceptable. It must hold significance to you though and you must be ready to part with or destroy the object yourself.

- [ ] A dildo or vibrator can be used sexually, if desired. Not required to have a nice time though. This will mainly be an extrasensory and strange bodily experience.

THE   RITUAL

1 For the best experience I recommend showering and meditating for 5-10 minutes beforehand. This is to put your body and mind in a relaxed state.

2 Brew your tea or boil hot water. It should be hot enough to enjoy drinking but eventually will end up on your body and your floor. I recommend something with a distinctive smell.

3 Begin with your initial invocation. You should be seated in a private space. If you are taking a substance that requires being held in your mouth begin it when the invocation starts. If it is something that is immediately swallowed, or smoked, eat it at the end of your invocation. This invocation is of my own design and written for the main recipient of this instructional manual. If in time you feel comfortable modifying the words to suit your own needs and spiritual practices, feel free. It is written in rhyming quatrains with irregular syllable counts based on poetics I know the recipient enjoys. Free verse or a shorter or longer form are both acceptable.

Invocation of and Submission to That Beyond Myself (to be read seated on the floor with your tea pot + vessel and candle + lighting implement in front of you and salt nearby, further physical instructions are as parentheticals).

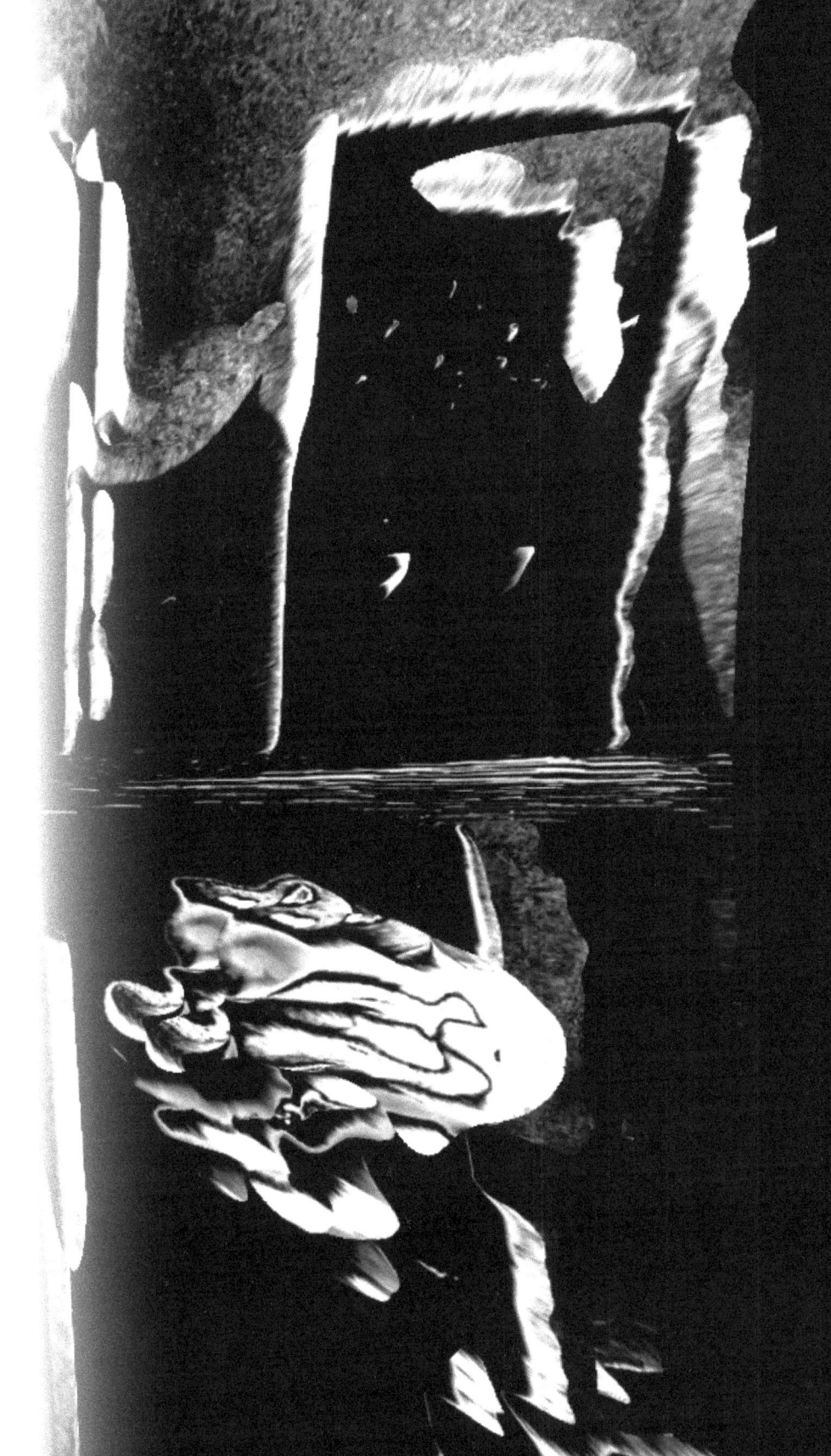

As I bring this tea and light
I ask for eyes beyond my sight

           (light candle)

To go beyond what's ill or right
And surrender to the conjured's might

(pour a small cup of tea, 1-2 fingers, you will need enough tea to draw symbols on the floor and dump some on yourself as you see erotically fit)

I bring this form fair and willing
Water and lust both meant for spilling

(dip two fingers into the tea and draw the shape of kano/kauna on your forehead, this is the norse rune of gateways and marks both your mind and body as an entrance point for spirits. ᚲ is what it looks like and you can see it more properly displayed in Unicode [here](.))

For no pleasure dares be as thrilling
To stand as wheat and ask for milling

(if your drug needs to be ingested do it now. Also take a small sip of the tea)

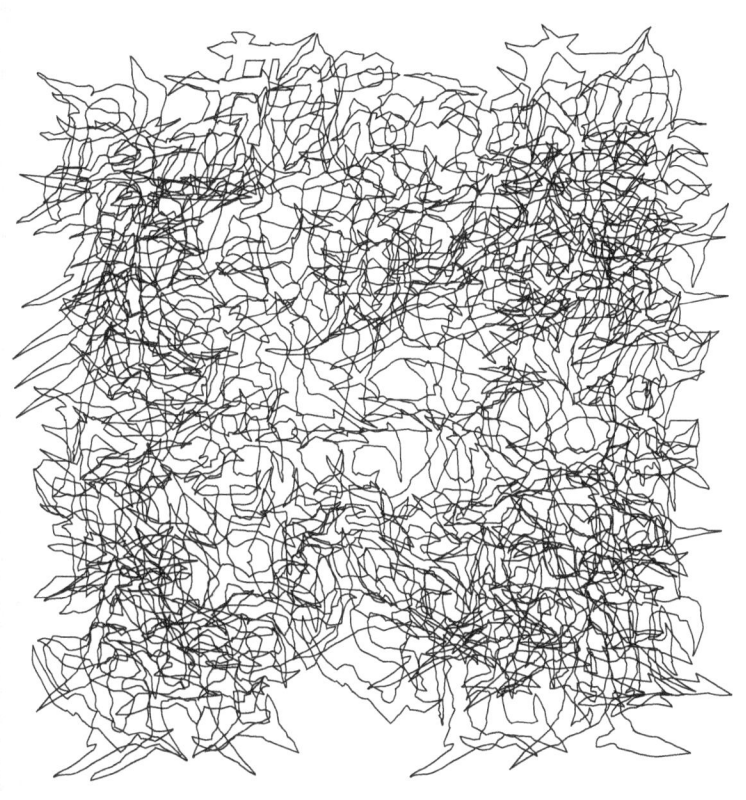

1 This part is now based around drawing diagrams. Stand and copy the figure of the appropriate President on the floor either around your candle and tea pot, or with enough space for you to sit within the inner circle. Choose from one of the following figures based on your needs or interests (this is a brief copy from Wikipedia but I highly recommend further researching each figure before committing). The appropriate symbol can be found in the full text of the Goetia on what is mysteriously labeled as 6 of 73 and has the phrase "SHEMHAMPHORASH" at the top of it (<https://archive.org/details/goetia_202006>).

> Barbas (or Marbas) is a demon described in the Ars Goetia. He is described as the Great President of Hell governing thirty-six legions of demons. He answers truly on hidden or secret things, causes and heals diseases, teaches mechanical arts, and changes men into other shapes. He is depicted as a great lion that, under the conjurer's request, changes shape into a man.

> Buer is a spirit that appears in the 16th century grimoire Pseudomonarchia Daemonum and its derivatives, where he is described as a Great President of Hell, having fifty legions of demons under his command. He appears when the Sun is in Sagittarius. Buer teaches Natural and Moral Philosophy, Logic, and the virtues of all herbs and plants. He also heals all infirmities, especially of men, and gives good familiars. He is depicted in the shape of Sagittarius, which is as a centaur with a bow and arrows. Additionally, Louis Le Breton created an illustration of Buer, later engraved by M. Jarrault, depicting the demon as having the head of a lion and five goat legs surrounding his body to walk in every direction. The etymology of his name is uncertain.

(Count/President) <u>Botis</u> (or Otis) is a Great President and Earl of Hell, commanding sixty legions of demons. He tells of all things past and future, and reconciles friends and foes. He is depicted as an ugly <u>viper</u>, but when he changes shape, he puts himself in human shape, with big teeth and two horns. When in human shape he carries a sharp and bright sword in his hand.

(Count/President) <u>Morax</u> (also Foraii, Marax and Farax) is a Great Earl and President of Hell, having thirty-six legions of demons under his command. He teaches <u>Astronomy</u> and all other liberal sciences, and gives good and wise <u>familiars</u> that know the virtues of all herbs and precious stones. He is depicted as a big <u>bull</u> with the face of a man. It has been proposed that Morax is related to the Minotaur which Dante places in Hell (Inferno, Canto xii). See Fred Gettings, Dictionary of Demons (1988) His name seems to come from Latin "morax", that delays, that stops.

(Count/President) Glasya-Labolas (also Caacrinolaas, Caassimolar, Classyalabolas, Glassia-labolis, Glasya Labolas, Gaylos-Lobos) is a mighty President of Hell who commands thirty-six legions of demons. He is the author and captain of manslaughter and bloodshed, tells all things past and to come, gains the minds and love of friends and foes causing love among them if desired, incites homicides and can make a man invisible. He is depicted as a dog with the wings of a <u>griffin</u>.

Foras (alternatively Forcas or Forrasis) is a powerful President of Hell, being obeyed by twenty-nine legions of demons.

- Not to be confused with Furcas.

- He teaches logic and ethics in all their branches, the virtues of all herbs and precious stones, can make a man witty, eloquent, invisible, and live long, and can discover treasures and recover lost things. He is depicted as a strong man. His name seems to derive from Latin foras (out, outside).

- The Thirty-first Spirit is Foras. He is a Mighty President, and appeareth in the Form of a Strong Man in Human Shape. He can give the understanding to Men how they may know the Virtues of all Herbs and Precious Stones. He teacheth the Arts of Logic and Ethics in all their parts. If desired he maketh men invisible, and to live long, and to be eloquent. He can discover Treasures and recover things Lost. He ruleth over 29 Legions of Spirits, and his Seal is this, which wear thou, etc.

- —S. L. MacGregor Mathers (1904)[22]

Malphas is a mighty Great President of Hell, having forty legions of demons under his command.

- Not to be confused with Malthus (demon).

- He builds houses, high towers and strongholds, throws down the buildings of the enemies, can destroy the enemies' desires or thoughts (and/or make them known to the conjurer) and all what they have done, gives good familiars, and can bring quickly artificers together from all places of the world. Malphas accepts willingly and kindly any sacrifice offered to him, but then he will deceive the conjurer. He is depicted as a crow that after a while or under request changes shape into a man, and speaks with a hoarse voice.

Haagenti (also Haage, Hage) is a Great President of Hell, ruling thirty-three legions of demons. He makes men wise by instructing them in every subject, transmutes all metals into gold, and changes wine into water and water into wine. Haagenti is depicted as a big bull with the wings of a griffin, changing into a man under request of the conjurer.

Camio (also Caim, Caym) appears in Ars Goetia, the first part of The Lesser Key of Solomon as a Great President of Hell, ruling over thirty legions of demons. Much detail is offered: he is a good disputer, gives men the understanding of the voices of birds, bullocks, dogs, and other creatures, and of the noise of the waters too, and gives true answers concerning things to come. He is depicted in 19th and 20th century occultist illustrations as appearing in the form of the black bird called a thrush, but soon he changes his shape into a man that has a sharp sword in his hand. When answering questions he seems to stand on burning ashes or coals. The title "President" of Hell would suggest a parallel with the presiding officer of a college or convocation, which are the only pre-modern uses of the term. Camio`s name seems to be taken from the biblical first murderer, Cain.

Ose (also Osé, Oze, Oso, Voso) is a Great President of Hell, ruling three legions of demons. He makes men wise in all liberal sciences and gives true answers concerning divine and secret things; he also brings insanity to any person the conjurer wishes, making him/her believe that he/she is the creature or thing the magician desired, or makes that person think he is a king and wearing a crown, or a pope. Ose is depicted as a leopard that after a while changes into a man. His name seems to derive from Latin «os", mouth, language, or "osor", that who abhors.

Amy (also Avnas) is the 58th spirit, a President of Hell,[6] and according to Johann Weyer's Pseudomonarchia daemonum:[23]

> ☒ Amy is a great president, and appeareth in a flame of fier, but having taken mans shape, he maketh one marvelous in astrologie, and in all the liberall sciences, he procureth excellent familiars, he bewraieth treasures preserved by spirits, he hath the government of thirtie six legions, he is partlie of the order of angels, partlie of potestats, he hopeth after a thousand two hundreth yeares to returne to the seventh throne: which is not credible.

Valac (also Ualac, Valak, Valax, Valu, Valic, Volac) is the mighty Great President of Hell, having thirty legions of demons under his command. Valac is said to give true answers about hidden treasures; he reveals where serpents can be seen, and delivers them harmless to the magician. He is said to appear as a small poor boy with angel wings riding on a two-headed dragon.

🗲 Now that you have drawn the diagram return to your seated position based on the scale and use the remaining tea as libations in the sense of a religious ritual and focus your attention on how it feels to physically pour the tea on your body. This can be done clothed or undressed as you see fit, but if you choose to strip it should be done so in a manner that you think would be sexually inviting to the entity of your choice while still reflecting your personality. What happens after this point will be highly personal and beyond the scale of what I can advise you regarding. You will simply know or be told what is to be done. Information for how to close the circle and return to your normal perception of reality will follow.

—

🕯 When you and the spirit are communing be sure to:

🕯 explicitly offer it your candle or other sacrifice and have a planned means of use or disposable you can enact during or after the ritual,

🕯 thank the spirit for whatever pleasures or wisdom it has given you and ask for permission to separate your experiences but know you are changed

🕯 when the time is appropriate, begin by again uttering your thanks while smelling, ingesting, or rubbing the salt on your person. This both grounds you in your physical reality and closes the gateway between you and the spirit. In case of emergency you can also always rely on the salt to close the gate between you.

🕯 Tap 3-5 times on your sternum as it feels pertinent or numerically appropriate to you as a way to return to the present. If the candle is still lit, extinguish it.

🕯 Recite the following: Our connection is closed but I carry your gifts, our return can come swiftly whenever I wish. Until you find yourself mentally grounded. You will know when this is.

🕯 Because of the variable length of time the ritual may take I recommend showering and relaxing after. Eat some solid food and hydrate more.

ℹ I have no real further comments at this time but once again urge people to take your psychological health and the subject matter seriously.

Demonology as Route to Unionization

or how to balance personal liberation with not merely being a lifestyle anarchist/leftist

brought to you by me kinning my vampire: the masquerade aka ronny midnight

THIS TEXT IS CREATIVE COMMONS /// GIVE THIS TO EVERYONE

in the first volume you missed:

how to fuck demons, a brief
overview of the ars goetia, &
safety warnings

WHAT DO WE HAVE IN STORE ?
—

- more safety warnings

- a brief overview on the history and problems of surveillance

- brief comments on time theft

- more demonology instructions

- how to not just think about shit but also do practical organizing

IT'S KINDA FUCKED THAT
WE ARE ALWAYS TORN
BETWEEN ACTION AND
INACTION

ON THE ONE HAND HAVING
AND DISTRIBUTING
INFORMATION IS RADICAL

ON THE OTHER HAND

SOMETIMES YOU JUST
HAVE TO SHUT THE FUCK
UP AND GO DO DISHES OR
GIVE THE HOMIE A RIDE
SOMEWHERE IN ORDER TO
DO POLITICS

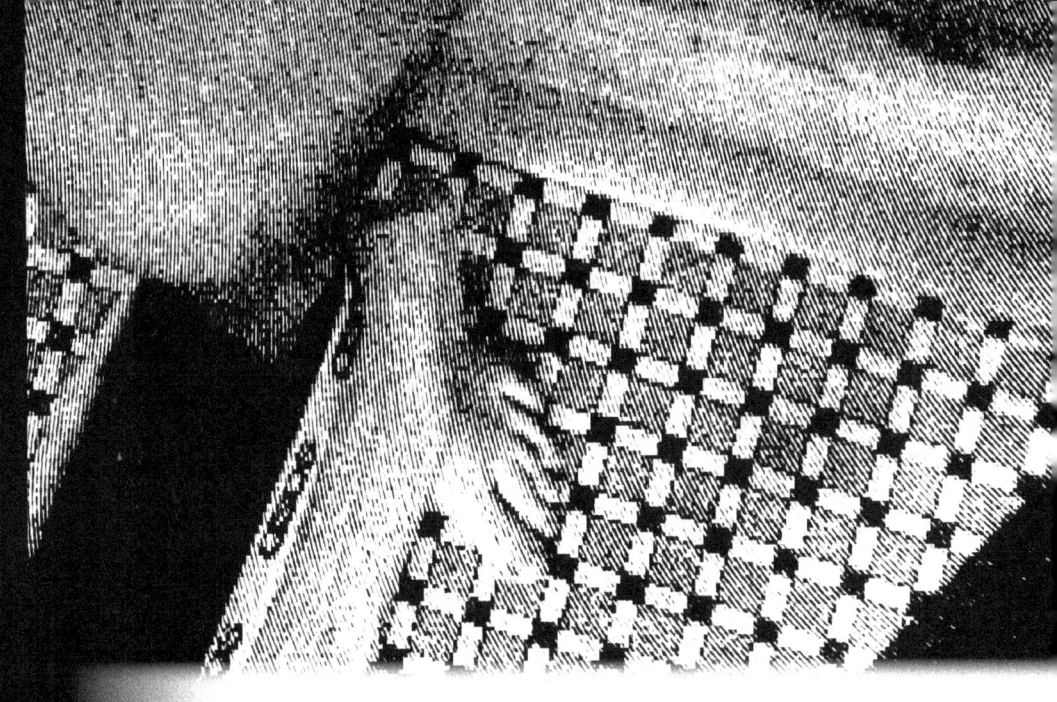

ACTUAL MATERIAL FORMS OF ANARCHISM USUALLY DON`T CONSIST OF THROWING BOMBS OR SINGLE ROMANTICIZABLE ACTIONS

ANARCHISM AND A TRUE COMMITMENT TO IT IS MOSTLY TEDIOUS AND BORING AND FRANKLY I WISH IT WAS COOLER AND I FEEL GUILTY THAT I`VE BEEN TOO TIRED FOR MUTUAL AID MEETINGS BECAUSE I WORK A SHITTY JOB

INSTEAD... I HAD A DEPRESSIVE SPELL WHERE I FUCKED AROUND AND REFUSED THE CONCEPT OF GOD OR PROGRESS THEN SOLD A BUNCH OF PRINTERS TO PEOPLE WHO DON`T NEED THEM

- 21 copies of volume 1 were given to a bunch of zoomers at a 100 gecs concert. I hope it fucked them up for life. nothing is arcane anymore. a world of verification and blue checks has removed all mystery.

The Disclaimers—

1 demonology and your results will be heavily determined by your mental state and should be used as a tool to bolster oneself and one`s will. rejecting oppressive regimes and celebrating or thriving in the face of marginalization—think of this as being "cast out" from a supposedly "good" society—is the prime intended use of these instructions. we are here to refuse gods and masters and/or only make ourselves beholden to those we approach gladly and of our own free will. if you found this language moving it is of both Dracula and anarchism alike. perhaps also the Addams family. sic gorgiamus allos subjectatos nunc.

2 combating stigma against drug use is important because of the racism in science and policing. addiction is also serious though and something I`ve struggled with myself. just as magic is a fine line that requires self-mastery, the use of psychedelics and other mind-altering substances should be taken with the gravity it deserves. all drug use in this pamphlet is strictly optional and all I ask in exchange for knowledge freely given is respect for your own safety. some information and thoughts on this shit:

> —naloxone, an opioid overdose preventer, can be gotten without a prescription at most pharmacies.

> —I promised my dad I would never do cocaine based on his own experiences and talking honestly. the PSAs are right. just talk openly about drug use.

— Nixon's war on drugs was an excuse to police people. the government introduces drugs into communities, plants drugs on people, and intentionally over-polices with regards to drugs.

— I feel like every five seconds we discover some new bullshit about organizations but the last I checked; the Sylvia Rivera Law Project is a good place to donate that would help people disproportionally affected by policing: https://slrp.org

☛ a big issue I've been debating is lifestyle anarchism and the draw of the occult. I read Bookchin's Social Anarchism or Lifestyle Anarchism (https://theanarchistlibrary.org/library/murray-bookchin-social-anarchism-or-lifestyle-anarchism-an-unbridgeable-chasm) and I am back and forth about his stance on occultism in leftist spaces. people who can't shut up about being a witch and their magic moonblood and shit are 1) annoying and drawing from something from the 70s as opposed to actual historical and cultural traditions and then get defensive when you point out it's from the 70s, 2) usually on some gender essentialist bullshit in a funny hat, and 3) replacing a potential for political action or an external gaze with internal growth. however, there's a sort of implied rejection of the "personal is political" as a mode of liberation and a lack of discussion of the sort of personal and spiritual liberation and racism and misogyny of supposed "rational" systems that are brought up in works such as Lorde's The Uses of the Erotic: The Erotic as Power and Gloria Anzaldúa's Borderlands/La Frontera. Most of the works that praise irrationality and mysticism that Bookchin cites are things like Gilles and Deleuze's various writings and Hakim Bey's T.A.Z. and nowhere in this does Bookchin really concern himself with race or gender as it intersects with these topics. all this to say, I think there's a middle ground between not getting distracted by internal liberation (especially when the person focusing on their liberation is mostly someone quite privileged) and using this new source of strength to both thrive in the face of destruction and as a source of energy in politically organizing. this is just a pamphlet that's supposed to be under 30 pages though and Bookchin's text is only 80-90 pages or so, so there's far more to be said about this topic than either of us can afford while keeping the text concise. either way, I think trusting people to find a balance and not just fall back into fetishism (the unfun kind), essentialism, or inaction is key.

BUT NOW ITS TIME TO MOVE ON !

and/or

HERE`S MORE CONTEXT I WROTE WHILE HIGH IN MY BATHTUB

*THE CAPITALIZATION WILL BE DIFFERENT HERE
& YOU SIMPLY HAVE TO ACCEPT THAT*

IF YOU DON`T LIKE IT >>> YOU CAN GET FUCKED

- I am resuming my notes in the dark. It is 1:05 am. Light from the courtyard shines through my bathroom window. I am running a bath. I have ingested edibles. I Could not tell you the dosage. When making anything from home i aim for doses ranging from 3 to 7 mg so that the average is 5 mg. I have a cooking scale for this purpose. The hot water works tension from my muscles. I am recording the segment by voice dictation.

I am suddenly an alarm. Perhaps an overview of the writing on surveillance I have done before this. My phone initially transcribed us as the writing of God, A deeply ironic confusion. The Panopticon, turn off the phone is what my phone initially transcribes, is as a god to lowly serfs such as us.

A constant state of surveillance asks us all not merely to be watched but also that which watches. I think of retail managers in similar terms, this is especially true of mid-level managers who have oversight of shifts but are not the general manager or assistant GM. They are in a state in which they still act as the hypothetical Boss of labor analysis, as well as are subjected to the boss, power. To become a manager is to become a self-devouring worm, but also affliction on fellow laborers. Managers are often fellow proletariat members who choose following economic compulsion and staying in line with the structures that promise rewards rather than building solidarity to deconstruct such things. This isn't to say that the existence of managers and bosses is good per se but just to reflect on their point in the chain as a strange and mirrored existence. They forgo the ability to build solidarity in exchange for a promise that always shortchanges them in terms of true social change but gives them an artificial sense of control and power. This isn't to say they don't have power over ground level employees but rather that that power is only bestowed to them by a higher structure which can arbitrarily change its whims and fancy. There is perhaps also a belief that one can be different with this power than others who wield it and perhaps in some of those cases it's even true if the sad individual is willing to sacrifice all their so-called perks for the benefit of those underneath them. All this to say the non-high-level manager is an interesting figure to analyze and is a parallel to the ways in which we all are both subject to and perpetuate social conditions.

There are times the retail employee is asked to enforce a policy. This policy will often intersect with a mode of oppression such as ableism (standing and sitting rules), perceived class or race-based profiling, transphobia, or any other interaction of the myriad of "undesirable" categories that now exist. Traditionally we may think the employee only has two options: to comply or to fully refuse. Often full refusal can be met with heavy opposition and/or termination. Depending on the employees, on experiences this may be a parallel form of oppression to that of the targeted person. The supposed HR apparatus exists to both accept complaints anonymously from employees and protect them from retaliation. His claim lines are usually ineffective at best or backfire/and or are actively malicious towards the whistleblower. Sometimes a viable strategy is to make it appear as if one is complying but in fact to do so ineffectively or not at all.

For example, if a manager asks one to give extra customer service to or follow a specific person in the store sometimes a viable choice may be to volunteer to do it and then explicitly say the person has done nothing wrong. This doesn't minimize the damage of the person experiencing being tailed in a store, but it also keeps the job from being done by someone who would make negative statements about said person. In an ideal world we would simply refuse the task and see those who ask for the task or called for it made to understand why such a thing is damaging. I understand that these gray-space answers that provide tools for working against a system while remaining covert are perhaps not the most noble or best version of the world or actions we could live with. Practically though having tools to do anything remotely subversive is still a plus.

The spells I have designed are both metaphorical tools to bolster one's confidence in their actions and spend time in planes of self-betterment mentally to resist work, as well as practical advice for how to go undetected in one's subversion. This is not to say one should avoid direct action, because as it is said it does get the goods, this is just a tool to help you choose your battles.

Smaller covert actions are often needed to build solidarity before committing to larger actions with one's coworkers and colleagues. Finding the balance of moves that is most effective in your workplace will be yours to master.

A FEW MONTHS AFTER WRITING THIS
I CAME OUT OF THE CLOUD THAT HAD COVERED ME

DUE TO THE WINTER MONTHS,
EXCESSIVE PSYCHEDELIC USE,
SEVERAL SOCIAL REJECTIONS,
& STARTING A NEW JOB
I FOUND MY MIND DISTORTED

WE WILL DISCUSS THE FIRST SPELL
WITH A WINTERY MIX OF OBSERVATIONS

1 CHOOSE A DEMON FROM THE ARS GOETIA. THIS BOOK WAS PROBABLY A SCAM TO GET PEOPLE TO BUY INGREDIENTS FROM SPECIFIC DUDES BUT THE TEXT HAS TAKEN ON A LIFE OF ITS OWN AND THAT IS WHAT GIVES IT POWER.

2 OK BUT HOW YOU CHOOSE THE DEMON IS BY LOOKING AT ITS DOMAINS AND ASKING YOURSELF WHAT YOU NEED THAT DAY

3 ON A DAY WHERE I MAY WISH TO CURSE THE STORE`S PROFITABILITY, I WOULD CALL ON HAAGENTI (48) TO TRANSMUTE THAT WHICH WOULD CAUSE FORTUNE TO BECOME THAT WHICH WOULD CAUSE RUIN. IT IS USUALLY BETTER TO FOCUS ON DEMON`S WHERE YOU ARE THE LOCUS OF THE ACTION. THINK AFFECTING YOUR VIEW OF YOUR COWORKER`S, GIVING YOU THE ABILITY TO COMPEL OTHER`S TO YOUR SIDE WHETHER THROUGH LOGOS OR ETHOS, OR BRINGING TOGETHER NEW FRIENDSHIPS.

4 LOOK AT THE SHAPES IN THE DEMON`S SIGILS AND PONDER THE LETTERS IN THEIR NAME. REDUCE THE SHAPES OR LETTERS TO A SINGLE/SIMPLER SHAPE WHICH MAY BE DRAWN IN THE AIR WITH YOUR FINGER OR SIMPLY HELD IN YOUR MIND.

5 AS YOU ARE FORCED TO WALK AROUND THE STORE OBSERVING, SELLING, REPORTING, STOCKING AND SO FORTH TRACE THE SYMBOL WITH YOUR FINGER AND HOLD IT IN YOUR MIND.

6 REPEAT THIS PROCESS AS FREQUENTLY AS POSSIBLE OR AS NEEDED

I spent two weeks doing this and can report the following results:

— it was easier to pass those two weeks by far. two weeks to two months is also the typical time it takes for me to exit a depressive spell. this ritual was a way to ground myself and pass time during work that would otherwise make me miserable.

— I found after 3 weeks I no longer needed to rely on this spell for day-to-day function

— it is a good way to look busy on camera while not being mentally present at work.

ℹ *NEXT: EXAMPLE PRAYERS AND ACTIONS YOU CAN TAKE IN YOUR WORKPLACE THAT HONOR THOSE PRAYERS*

MAY BAEL MAKE ME INVISIBLE TO MY ENEMIES

> IF YOU SEE SOMEONE SHOPLIFTING
>> OR A COWORKER BREAKING A RULE
>>> YOU HAVE NOT IN FACT SEEN ANYTHING

MAY AGARES FOSTER NEW CONNECTIONS AND BRING STAND-STILLS TO AN END

> https://www.iww.org/organize/
>> I HAVE ATTEMPTED TO FORM A UNION AND FAILED SO I GET THAT THIS IS SPOOKY
>>> TALK ABOUT THE UNION LEADERS STARBUCKS FIRED IN MEMPHIS
>>>> I ALSO RECOMMEND MAKING IMPROVEMENTS TO YOUR BREAK ROOM AND POINTING OUT TO YOUR COWORKERS THIS IS SOMETHING THE STORE YOU WORK FOR EASILY COULD HAVE AFFORDED AS A RADICALIZATION TALKING POINT

MAY VASSAGO BRING TRUTH TO LIGHT

> TALK ABOUT WAGE DESCREPENCY AND KNOW YOUR RIGHTS REGARDING IT
>> SUPPORT YOUR COLLEAGUES AND PROTECT THEM FROM RETALIATION

A / S A C R I F I C E / T O / M A L P H A S

THE THIRTY-NINTH SPIRIT IS MALPHAS. HE APPEARETH AT FIRST LIKE A CROW, BUT AFTER HE WILL PUT ON HUMAN SHAPE AT THE REQUEST OF THE EXORCIST, AND SPEAK WITH A HOARSE VOICE. HE IS A MIGHTY PRESIDENT AND POWERFUL. HE CAN BUILD HOUSES AND HIGH TOWERS, AND CAN BRING TO THY KNOWLEDGE ENEMIES' DESIRES AND THOUGHTS, AND THAT WHICH THEY HAVE DONE. HE GIVETH GOOD FAMILIARS. IF THOU MAKEST A SACRIFICE UNTO HIM HE WILL RECEIVE IT KINDLY AND WILLINGLY, BUT HE WILL DECEIVE HIM- THAT DOTH IT. HE GOVERNETH 40 LEGIONS OF SPIRITS, AND HIS SEAL IS THIS, ETC.

🜚 you will need a post-it note or a small piece of paper. a writing implement. spitting.

🯱 MALPHAS IS A LIAR. ALL BOSSES ARE LIARS. PREPARE YOURSELF TO BE DECEIVED BUT GLADLY AND ON YOUR OWN TERMS.

🯲 INSCRIBE THE SIGIL OF MALPHAS UPON YOUR PAPER AND SPEAK THE FOLLOWING: MALPHAS I OFFER THE GIFT OF LIFE. I OFFER THE MOISTURE WHICH MAKES ME AND IS FROM WHICH I CRAWLED FORTH.

🯳 SPIT UPON THE INSCRIPTION AND TRACE THE SHAPE AGAIN WITH YOUR FINGER.

🯴 MALPHAS WILL ACCEPT THIS GLADLY AND OF HIS VOLITION. YOU MAY NOW ASK ONE FAVOR OF HIM:

> 🯅 good concepts for favors: health of nearby animals, physical safety and stability, improved reliability of work equipment

> 🯆 ill-advised favors: requests for information, curses upon enemies, anything that could remotely backfire

🯵 THIS SPELL WORKS BEST IF THE REMAINING PAGE CAN BE SECRETED OR WEDGED SOMEWHERE AND KEPT ON PREMISES

5 IS THE NUMBER AND THE NUMBER IS 5

TRACE THE SHAPE OF A STAR

COUNT TO 5

MERCURY IS THE PLACE OF TRANSFORMATION

YOU ARE RESPONSIBLE FOR THE TRANSFORMATION OF AETHER TO EARTH

1 FIND A COWORKER IN NEED AND SUPPORT THEM

2 FIND A COMMUNITY MEMBER OR FRIEND IN NEED AND SUPPORT THEM

3 IF YOU ARE IN NEED TRY THE FOLLOWING

    a 3 AND A HALF CUPS FLOUR

    b 1 CUP WATER

    c ONE PACKET OR TEASPOON OF INSTANT YEAST

    d ADJUST WITH WATER AND FLOUR UNTIL A SHAGGY TEXTURE

    e 25 MINUTES AT 325 F

    f EAT

4 DO NOT REPORT LOITERING CUSTOMERS. IF YOU SEE SOMETHING FORGET IT.

5 FORGETTING IS THE PANACEA.

UNIONS AND FORMS OF ORGANIZATION CAN BE CORRUPTED BY PEOPLE WITHIN THEM WHO ARE MOTIVATED BY GREED OR POWER ETC BUT ALSO, THEY ARE ONE OF THE FEW TOOLS WE HAVE AGAINST THE PROVERBIAL BOSS SO USE THEM

- the hardest part of organizing is the fear wielded by corporations

  for any growth done through this zine to mean anything you must also turn ether to earth, self-realization to action.

oh shit
oh fuck
you wanna read more?

no swag
all luck
see what's in store

choak.wtf

may that which guide you
never be binding—
or at least may your miseries
not be without consent.

— senia hardwick,
fall 2021/winter 2022

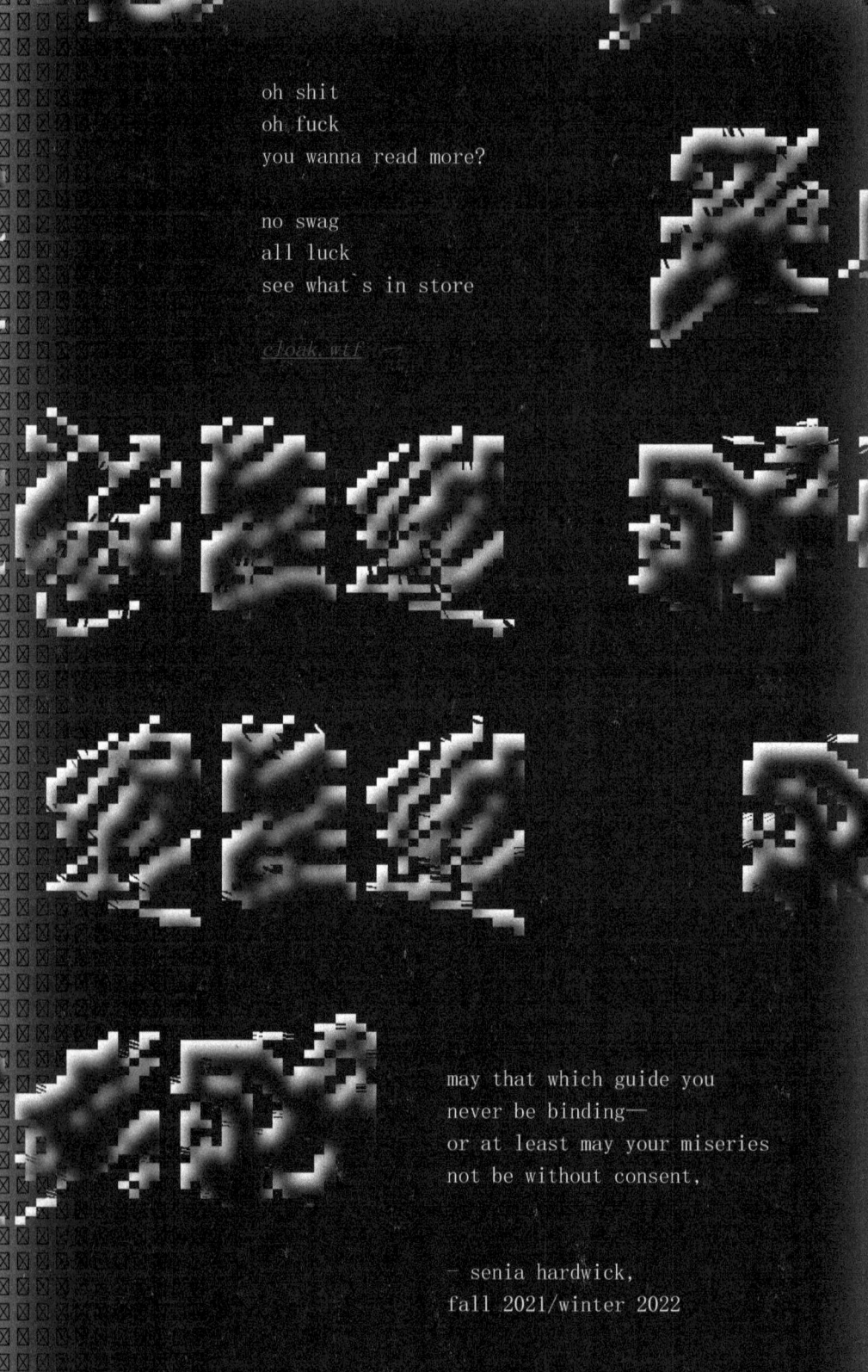

A GIFT GIVEN & A GIFT RECEIVED

or Divination using the Ars Poetica and a
Reflection on the Eroticism of a Virtual Re...
Guillotine

A GIFT GIVEN & A
GIFT RECEIVED

THIS TEXT IS CREATIVE COMMONS /// GIVE THIS TO EVERYONE

in the first volume you missed:

how to fuck demons, a brief overview of the ars goetia, & safety warnings

in the second volume you missed:

how to counter retail surveillance, time theft, demonology instructions, & practical organizing

Divination

In the previous pamphlets I have written to you all as various personas adopted by a vampire wizard I made up. The desire is to be the most myself in this volume. But in its transcription, I too cannot help becoming a persona. Autobiography is not fiction, but it is LARPing.

Using the Ars Goetia and a Reflection on the Eroticism of a Virtual Reality Guillotine

However, my name is Senia. I was named for a Slavic man who saved his family from waves of violence. His ancestors too resisted waves of violence. For most of us to be here, our ancestors have survived waves of violence. Unfortunately, sometimes (I held my breath here, a pause for effect please dear reader) ⋯ unfortunately, sometimes, they were also the wave.

❶ 3/6/22 — Hear ye, hear ye and welcome to the future. My previous issues in this series are on the basics of summoning a demon to fuck and an introduction to thinking about unionization. *MIKE* from *CLOAK* has very nicely invited me to do a third pamphlet. It is between 5 and 7am as I write this, or rather I wager that`s how long I`ll be up. I start around 5:30 to ponder a reflection I wrote on the guillotine that I had lost, and the directions I had promised for my friend from the first pamphlet.

The concept here is to reflect on one gift I am giving (how to preform divination with coins themed to the Ars Goetia) and one gift I have received (another friend let me simulate chasing them down and executing them in a virtual reality world—a sexual fantasy I would and could not simulate in real life). So much of these pamphlets has been about desire and simulation.

The more time passes and the more I come to understand the world, the more Baudrillard`s statements on the simulacra and the signifier and the signified make sense to me. For the unfamiliar, I will summarize. For the curious, I will include the following:

> ❶ http://mysite.du.edu/~tweaver2/artd2355/schedule/baud_sim.pdf

> ❷ https://archive.org/search.php?query=baudrillard

There is something that is real, be it power, money, culture, an art object or a person, and in encountering capitalism (according to Baudrillard) or in the need to be communicated (my interpretation/extrapolation of the text, this is a debatable point), a stand-in for this true thing is created. Capitalism does this to enforce both itself and something Baudrillard calls hyperreality, whereas human communications often turn ideas into memes, metaphors, archetypes or signifiers. The word signifier here is a bit loaded, as I'm stealing it from Jean-Paul here, but Baudrillard calls that which is true and being evoked by an idea the signified and the thing that is a copy or mimic of it, the signifier.

Or in the words of Kaiki Deishuu, "The fake is stronger than the real. In its deliberate attempt to be real, it's more real than the real thing."

While the appropriation of reality by capitalism is clearly negative, I don't think the human capacity to make new cultural realities is always inherently negative. It's dangerous for sure, but all culture, ideology, and language can be used to destroy. As a trans person and a somewhat insane one at that, I've come to stop worrying about what in my presentation is fake or real by reminding myself that while I'm not fake, in my deliberate exploration and indication/signaling of various aspects of identity and gender presentation, I am becoming more of what I am indicating than the expected or original impulse. In choosing to signify masculinity through a choice of a certain watch or glasses or how I fold my shirtsleeves, I am reflecting that my own core holds more masculinity than some cultural notion that also requires a tyrannical slavishness—a contractual bind to a toxic masculinity. This is not to take a Butlerian stance that gender is merely performed, but rather a strategy using performance to bolster one's inner confidence.

I am not really that concerned with Lucifer as he's kind of a very Christian demon and at this point, I've become more interested in demons entirely separate of the concept of them rebelling against Christ/God/*All That Nonsense*. I had a phase where I was a little more set to attack and dethrone God and so forth, but I prefer to not really give them (Christians and their ideology) the time of day now as a further rebellion. Yes, we are worshipping demons. No, it's not about you anymore. Taking demons from them and making them a stranger and more intrinsic thing separate of their supposed truthful origin feels fitting.

I brought up Lucifer because taking up aspects of cultural practice while refusing the negative ones is a powerful move.

This is an example of or heavily influenced by Muñoz` [concept of disidentifcation](). José Esteban Muñoz describes the processes by which subjects, especially queer people of color, rework objects or cultural signs to have new cultural meaning, especially objects or cultural signs related to their own cultural histories and oppression. All language and culture are alchemical, and in manipulating its pieces we create something even larger than what we started with. Words and letters itself reflect this wizardry. Mamoud Darwish describes the magic of language as, "lethargic letters, which carry no value when separate, build a house when they come together." It is worth mentioning this is experience is especially true in Arabic and other languages where the full meaning of the phrase cannot be known until its read and its entirety (*In the Presence of Absence*).

[7:28am the will is gone. I`ve been writing for two hours. I will go back to sleep now. Find the book on the shelf later. I will remember the guillotine feeling and knife gifts for part 2 and to draw a diagram for part 1. I`m scared I`m going to lose some essential fragment by stopping, but I can trust in my ability to return. It`s too early to be up. My husband is leaving for work.]

(I have often found many people younger than myself seem to know less about piracy than I`d expect. Archive.org is an incredible font of knowledge. JSTOR now also allows you free articles. While we`re discussing such things, I also recommend [Sci-Hub]() and [Project Gutenberg]())

3/10/22— The memory of what I initially wrote on the Guillotine is almost gone. A couple days after executing a sexual/D/s play partner in virtual reality, I scrawled several reflections on that into my phone and accidentally deleted the draft. I'm doing my best to recall the major shapes. It's 5:21pm on a Thursday.

I suppose the first essential piece of information is that I feel a desire toward decapitation that has developed over time. I've been terribly fascinated by martyrdom images since I was a teenager and read *Confessions of a Mask* by Yukio Mishima, an exploration of a young man's increasingly violent homosexual fantasies which is largely tied to Mishima's unfortunately radical politics (https://archive.org/details/confessionsofmas00mish_0). A long series of morbid fascinations pre-dated this text, but the odd synchronicity of both the narrator and I discovering our sexuality by our physical separation from other men cemented something within me.

For the sake of their privacy, we will refer to my companion in this virtual enterprise as Viola.

Viola and I regularly use a virtual reality program, themselves with a headset and myself with simply a laptop and standard interface. For a previous social event, I had researched if there were any functioning guillotines available to visit in the various digital worlds people made. As you likely expect, the answer is yes.

Viola went ahead of me into the world environment and invited me while they had a chance to hide. They also found a knife that exists in the world and left it for me. This knife is an equippable object that when you strike another player in the world with it, they are instantly transported to the guillotine, and one simply has to press the button to see them executed.

[~~MIKE I HAVE EMAILED YOU A PICTURE OF THE GUILLOTINE AND THE PROFILE OF THE PERSON WHO MADE IT~~]

The execution itself is an illusion. The user's avatar lays along the flat back of the guillotine and when the blade drops, their avatar drops as well—when standing at the right angles one simply sees their head drop accompanied by the sound of the blade and a delightfully wet, and likely to some users, nauseating thud.

The gift I have received was not only the opportunity to safely indulge an otherwise inactable fetish, but also that of an invitation.

an invitation hovering

rusted   chest height

"find me"   "chase me"

yellow blade   rusted veins   silent hill x soul edge

my blade x your neck

slipping up

shipping us

find you in the walls   with thousands of women   beneath jaundiced paper

an invitation hovering

rusted   chest height

"find me"   "chase me"

yellow blade   rusted veins   silent hill x soul edge

my blade x your neck

slipping up

shipping us

find you in the walls   with thousands of women   beneath jaundiced paper

an invitation hovering

rusted   chest height

"find me"   "chase me"

yellow blade   rusted veins   silent hill x soul edge

my blade x your neck

slipping up

shipping us

beneath jaundiced paper   find you in the walls   with thousands of women

- [3/18 return to knife poems, smoking a mix of rose petals and marijuana, coffee with oat milk, afternoon, trying to not get too buzzed from any substance and trying listening to ASMR mic scratching sounds for focus, USB keyboard plugged into laptop (her name is Leila for the curious), hope to get through three of them, music playing is "<u>hard chiptune mix 2</u>". ~~To both Mike for the formatting~~ and all those who might doubt me, the next poem is justified.]

1

the first knife a woman gave me was from my abusive ex-girlfriend.
the first time a girl let me touch her, I could do nothing but choke her.
          my relationship with women has been largely disordered.
              at their own request.

  I am aware how this sounds.   I have been told how it sounds.
I am not sure of the level of autobiography I wish to include in my own work anymore.

this will be hard for MIKE to format. let's return to the fantasy.

where has the head gone? where is its writer? ubi sunt qui ante nos in hoc mundo fuere? I will ask this as many times as I have to. now come out of the walls, so I can cut your fucking head off.

2

there is a space in reality where I sit at my computer. there is a space in my computer that renders information visually. there is a space in the virtual that takes us both to a hospital.

in the center of a hospital is a lobby space and in the center of that space is a guillotine.

it goes. jetz und jetz.

j`écris ces lignes. il est 6 h 10.

it is the last execution   but instead I am murdering my lover.

I am frequently terrified by my own desires.
    not that I'd act on them.   but that it marks a fundamental separation
        between society and me.
           bifurcated: thought from action   self from other

head from shoulders.

            I want s(t)imulation   but with a soft core beneath
    I will put on my wristwatch   and call you an ingrate
        and wish to be cradled   post fallen gleam.

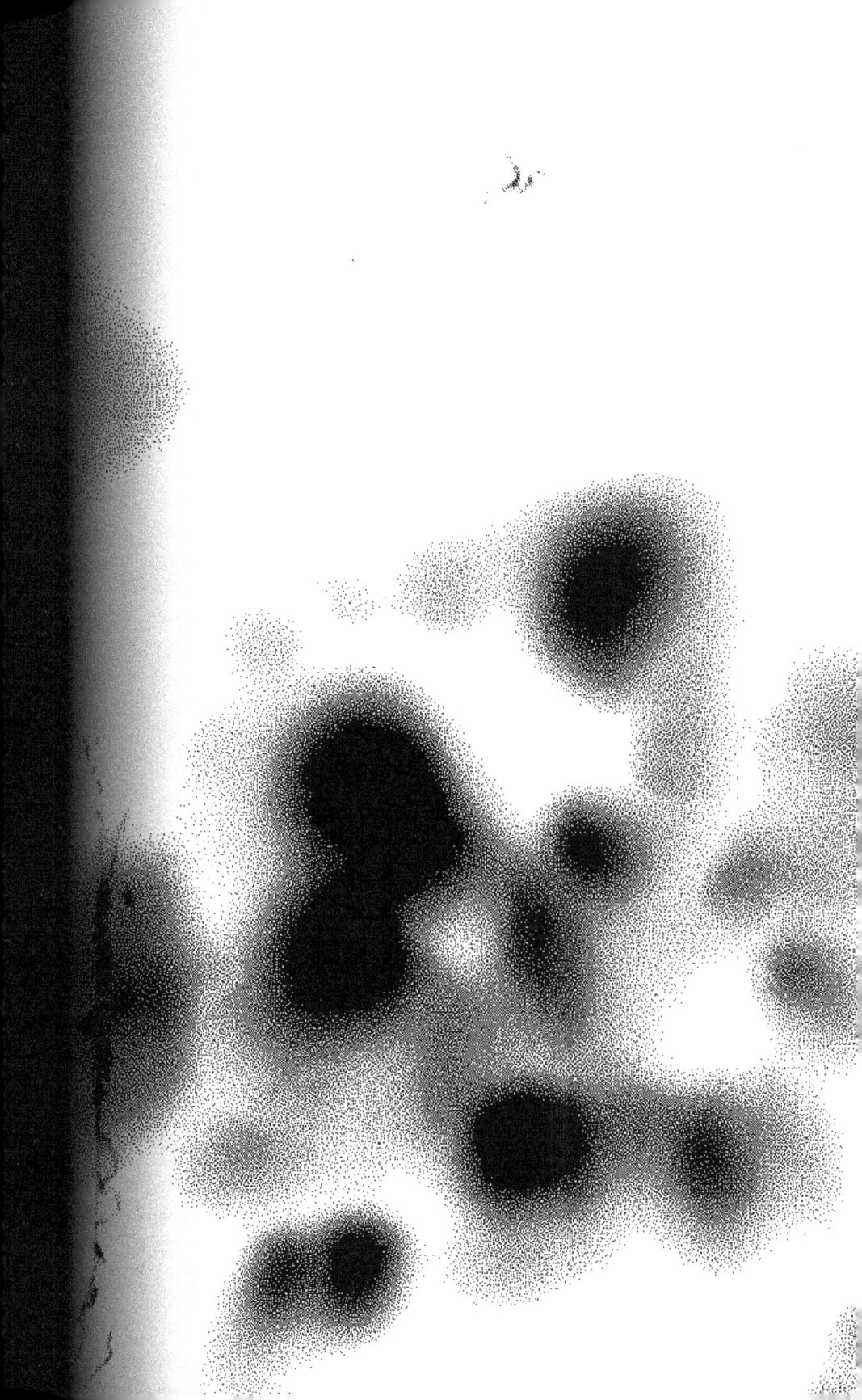

[3/20 I decided I should write one more poem to maintain the sets of three... then I tried to... and I think I've said what needs to be said... Oh, the irregularity of satisfaction!]

- before we break into the divination... I wanted to include some comments from a friend regarding the first pamphlet in this series:

  > ☐ closing the connection might feel emotionally difficult, depending on how things went, your personal temperament, etc. it definitely was for me! trying to really internalize the final words helped me a lot. I guess I would say, find any way you can to remind yourself that this isn't the end, and you've created something that lasts - it's true! and it makes it easier.

  an essential part of any magic is creating the liminal space (both mentally and physically) that the ritual occurs in. magic is not so much a literal manipulation of forces but rather an alchemy of personal symbols and psychologies, rendering one the Magician (in the tarot sense) of one's own life.

  the Magician converts ether and thought into action; turning wands and cups to pentacles and swords, while a lemniscate crowns him as the master of Gestalt. Gestalt is a pattern, form, or shape that is both defined by and surpasses its components. as a psychological/philosophical practice it began in Germany in the early 20th century and is still used in contemporary frameworks (<u>https://en.wikipedia.org/wiki/Gestalt_psychology</u>).

  again—as previously discussed regarding Munoz and Darwish—all psychology and culture is alchemy and all alchemy, be it literal or metaphorical, is based around the manipulation of parts that surpass the whole. in this instance, by creating an opening and closing practice, Florence was able to reduce/manage their anxieties regarding both abandonment and a fear of the summoned entity feeling abandoned or disregarded. the application of ritual served as a reminder of the continuous nature of experience and the delight of possibility.

if you find yourself needing more of a closing
or opening practice; I would encourage exploring
different modes of engaging the senses such as:

- aromas (I have included links to small businesses from my area if you do not have reasonable access to purchasing or foraging such things)
    - https://flowerpower.net/product-category/bulk-herbs/
    - https://brooklyntea.com/collections/best-sellers

- ambient soundscapes (I would discourage anything with too much narrative or lyricism to it but to each their own)
    - recommending these gets weird because there`s a lot of appropriative material in the world of meditation and music for meditation but I tried to find things that are not fucked
    - https://www.youtube.com/watch?v=xNN7iTA57jM
    - https://www.youtube.com/watch?v=3sLOomwE1xw

- the 54321 senses dbt skill
    - https://copingskillsforkids.com/blog/2016/4/27/coping-skill-spotlight-5-4-3-2-1-grounding-technique

[MIKE: I THINK SOME SORT OF BREATH/IMAGE LAYOUT HERE COULD BE NICE? I FEEL A VERY NATURAL]

Numismatomancy with the Ars Goetia

Numimatomancy is the word for divination using coins from the Greek nomisma (coins) and manteia (prophecy). Coins have a variety of significance throughout the world; in the case of the Greeks, coins were placed over the eyes of the dead in order to pay Charon, the boatman who ferries souls across the River Styx. A similar tradition exists in Ukranian culture, where coins are placed on the eyes and tongue of the dead to prevent them from bringing another living soul as payment. A popular method of the I Ching uses coins to generate the hexagrams of the King Wen Sequence.

Different metals are associated with various planets and metaphysical categories, but coins generally are associated with the afterlife, earth, physical health and material wealth in a variety of western cultures.

Runecasting is also a popular practice though this historicity of various rituals:
https://en.wikipedia.org/wiki/Runic_magic

The coins this process is written for are available here, but they cost $80:
https://www.etsy.com/listing/1186012557/goetia-coin-set-all-72-demon-seals

Alternatively, I recommend instead numbering 72 pennies.

—

The Ars Goetia can be found [here](#).

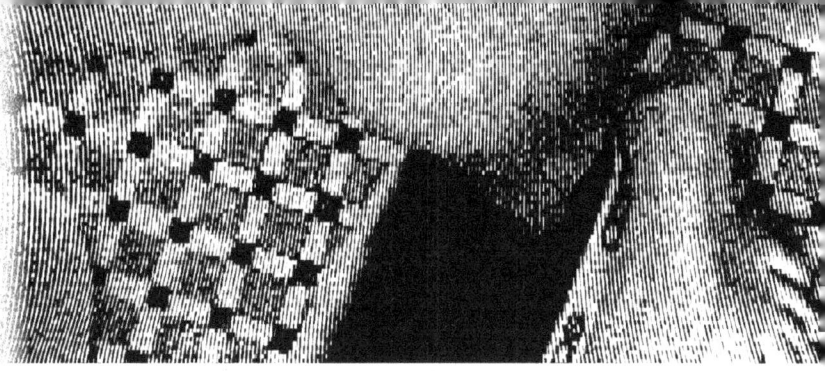

The first part of the process is creating the diagram for casting the coins. Observing the following diagram will be more practical than my describing the various charts, but in the case of e-readers I will do my best to describe it. This can be done on a sheet of paper, but in my case I have a plank of wood I reuse that has a pentagram inscribed on the other side that I have affectionally nicknamed my "witchboard," despite self-identifying more as a wizard. Witchboard frankly sounds cooler.

The overall diagram consists of four concentric circles, the first two being the magic circle and a smaller circle around it to denote space for labeling the planets. In the center of the circle is a similar divider/labeling ring and smaller circle. Then within the main "donut" shaped portion of the magic circle, 9 divisions should be drawn for each of the now accepted planets and Pluto who we still love, respect, and include in this zine.

The inner circle is then inscribed with the alchemical symbol for the sun, and the inner segments are then labeled with the planets and Pluto in order of their proximity to the sun. I have also included examples of each symbol outside the diagram and information about what each planet relates to ideologically and metaphysically. These are less refined summaries and more personal impressions, I would encourage you to do your own research in this regard.

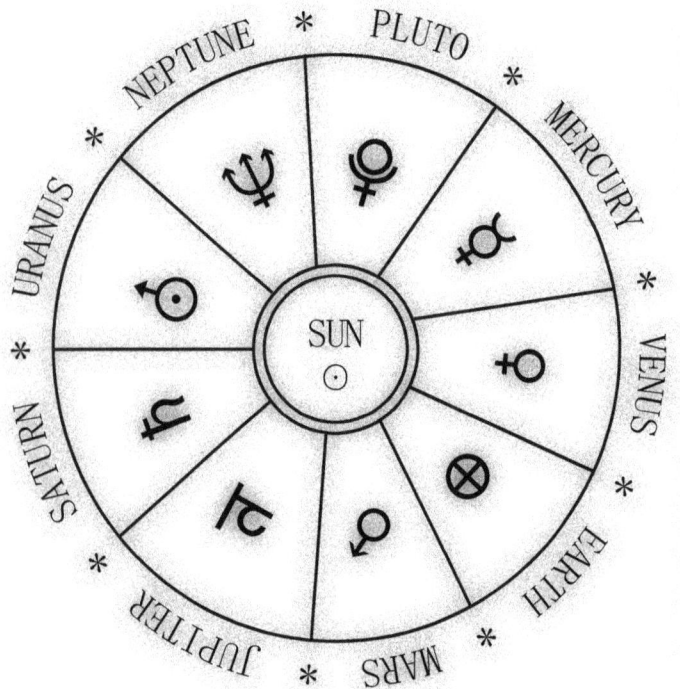

The Sun

☉ - 19 in the Tarot, the Sun, fire, the self - life, healing, masculine and feminine energy alike in various cultures, rebirth - gold, the refined spirit - the blackened sun is a symbol of decomposition and is the first step in making the Philosopher's Stone, it is also a symbol for the Shadow Self, that which we hide from ourselves - Leo

Mercury

☿ - affiliated with air in astrology but water in alchemy, quicksilver, communication, and Virgo + Gemini - Castor and Pollux, Hermes - the smallest planet yet also closest to the sun - gathering information - sulfur and salt, the trinity of creation, creativity and opportunity

Venus

♀ - love, intimate communications, messengers, the divine feminine if that's empowering for you - the slowest rotation around the sun but the hottest temperatures - water, Taurus and Libra - passion, sensuous energy, copper - finding pleasure in service to or service from others - I associate Venus with The Lovers in the Tarot

Earth

♁ OR the symbol on the diagram [~~MIKE: I prefer mine but for some reason the unicode is not supported???, if we can insert the symbol as a graphic let me know~~] - grounded temperments and people, nurturing, material wealth, in some cultures the feminine - the root or origin of a situation OR the beginning of one's journey - in this way I associate it with The Fool (the journey's beginning) and Strength from the Tarot - the unity of elements - the concept of Gestalt

Mars

♂ - Conflict both external and internal, transformative anger - Tuesdays, iron, war, masculine energy - Ares and Scorpio in Astrology - rams, blood sacrifice, reaping what one sews - action coming to a head - the King of Swords, fire, gay sex - passion, determination, ambition, visions of a way forward

Jupiter

♃ - fatherhood/paternal figures, augury, oxen and the sacrifice there of - the Norse rune Dagaz, exploration of ideas, good luck - lightning, mentors, intergenerational wealth and knowledge, Sagittarius and Pisces

Saturn

♄ - Capricorn and Aquarius, time - the story of Kronos, putting one's nose to the grind, earth - control, finesse, difficulty receiving or handling emotions - lead, the beginning of one's alchemical journey - The Emperor (personal and subjective choice)

Uranus

♅ - Aquarius, Air, the sky - platinum, The Magician, electric blue (the color) - new ideas and cultural revolution, sudden change - technology, freedom, authenticity - transformation in the face of chaos, unexpected possibilities

Neptune

Ψ – water, the oceans, Pisces – the Wheel of Fortune, the change of the tides, creativity, the King of Cups – the meeting of the material and the ethereal/the connection between the spirit and body – artistic self-expression, inspiration, sacrifice that drives growth – mysticism and enchantment

Pluto

♇ – Scorpio, the realm of the dead, transformation and the occult, sensuous energy – hidden knowledge, The High Priestess – depravity and pleasure seeking (good here), orgasms, obsession, psychoanalytic theory – the subconscious and that which is inherited both literally and psychologically from one`s parents.

BEGINNING THE DIVINATION ITSELF

We begin by **Opening the Circle**. You should have your coins in some manner of container and your planetary board drawn. Sit before the board and hold the bag of coins (etc) in your dominant hand. For those curious, the following is a **villanelle** (*https://en.wikipedia.org/wiki/Villanelle*). I wrote this for my friend who fucks demons so if you don't want to pay the demons with sex, here are some words that can replace flesh depending on how you do worship: blood, song, art.

RECITE THE FOLLOWING:

I open my mind to all that could be
Whether it's chaos or the strings of fate
The past and the future are mine to see

I ask of you spirits to hear my plea¬¬
Come forth and match my will to liberate
I open my mind to all that could be

I'll eat of knowledge's forbidden tree
For I have no fear of Abaddon's gate
The past and the future are mine to see

I know that no gifts are given for free
Moving the scales calls forth the counterweight
I open my mind to all that could be

By coins and flesh I'll gladly pay the fee
Whether the repayment is small or great
The past and the future are mine to see

In faith I'll render what you'd have of me
The real is defined by what we create
I open my mind to all that could be
The past and the future are mine to see

Now for the casting of the coins. Draw a small handful of coins and drop them above the center of the board. I would recommend using 3-9 coins though there's no right or wrong way to grab them.

You then should consult the **Ars Goetia** on the domains of each demon and interpret them as read through the planet's domain they land on. **For example...**

Casting **Valefar** in the place of **Jupiter** would mean an intersection of **thieves or traitors** with issues of **fortune and mentors**. It could mean to watch for a betrayal by a parental or mentor figure or people looking to take advantage of one's good luck.

Casting **Forneus** in the place of **Neptune** would mean an intersection of **language and communication skills** and **creativity**. This is an auspicious time to create new ideas and calls for connecting oneself and others to their higher purpose.

After reflecting on your casting comes **the closing of the circle**. During your reflection you may wish to photograph, record, or journal on your findings. You begin the closing ritual by returning the coins to their vessel. As you do so **recite the following:**

With council fair comes fair the fee
The wheel does turn and so does fate
I won't cast off what's asked of me
My future self is far too great

I've done my time now close the gate
The door is shut but I still see
All bridges have their counterweight
My will defines what fate will be

❶ **To a certain extent...** the existence of this zine series is owed to David Lowery's *The Green Knight*. I had greatly anticipated the film as someone who many of the concepts in *Sir Gawain & The Green Knight* have an erotic charge.

The relationship between host and guest, the tension of morality and obligation, a beautiful young man who can eb beheaded yet never die—all these things are sexually charged dynamics. The promise of a more openly psychosexual interpretation of the work filled me with anticipation.

> Now swear me here with truth to keep this `twixt us twain
> Whate`er our hap may be, or good or ill befall.

The movie still speaks to me on several levels even with the criticisms I have of it. Or as I have more superficially put it on a variety of `blue hellsites:` this is just a casual reminder Sir Gawain is in fact my boyfriend.

> Let us swear, friend, to make this exchange,
> however our hap may be, for worse or for better.

On discovering the tie-in tabletop roleplaying game, I suffered a horrible bout of purchaser's madness and acquired it immediately.

I then ran a tabletop game with a few friends that was a catalyst for a friend to start running his own games. I was invited to join a table of *Vampire: The Masquerade*, a modern gothic horror setting in which players assume the role of vampires, and Ronny Midnight was born.

—

In short, Ronny is a 1970s Satanist who becomes a vampire. In learning of actual modes of enlightenment and gaining supernatural power, he loses and inflicts the loss of what he values most on other's around him, free will.

In creating Ronny, I opened my own history with studying the occult, surviving emotional abuse, and interest in music and science fiction history. I also did a decent number of psychedelics, struggled with a winter depressive episode, and built both new and old friendships.

As a vampire, Ronny has lived under several pseudonyms, drifting in and out of the goth/occult scene of NYC since the 1950s. Previous identities include Danny D'Orias and Pyxis the Navigator. Pyxis comes from Pyxis Nautica, a constellation depicting a mariner's compass. Beneath the layer of Pyxis exists Ronny and beneath Ronny exists me. As the zine series progresses the layers of roleplayed self are removed. Or as said in the perhaps questionable of me to reference film, *Tropic Thunder*, "the dudes are emerging."

In spending time thinking about playing Ronny, I returned to several works on the occult I had been passionate about in my youth. I was reminded of why I was interested in it back then and rediscovered new ways to relate to the work now. When the recipient of the first issue lamented their inability to fuck a demon, this project was born of my offhanded, but well-meaning response, "you know I could tell you how to do that right?"

I've also been on my own rather rapid journey of self-discovery and recovery simultaneous to the creation of these three zines largely due to a series of other events related to the ripple of *The Green Knight*.

I've been quite grateful to Mike, my readers, and friends who have encouraged me along this process.

See you in the ether,

-SH

CLOAK

WRITTEN BY
DESIGNED BY

SENIA HARDWICK
CLOAK

www.ingramcontent.com/pod-product-compliance
Lightning Source LLC
Chambersburg PA
CBHW062053290426
44109CB00027B/2814